D1194884

SOME IMPORTANT PLACES IN THE BEATLES' LIVES

1. Liverpool, England. John Lennon, Paul McCartney, George Harrison, and Ringo Starr were all born in Liverpool. While growing up, they all loved rock and roll music, which was just becoming popular at the time.

2. Hamburg, Germany. When they were starting out as a group, the Beatles often traveled to Hamburg, where they played in small music clubs. It was an important experience because this is where the Beatles found and developed their own special music style.

3. London, England. London is the capital of England. The Beatles spent much of their time there, writing and recording music. They set up their own record company in London called Apple Corps.

4. United States. In 1964, the Beatles traveled to New York City. They were greeted by thousands of cheering fans and news reporters. They appeared on a popular TV show where millions of Americans saw them for the first time. This was the beginning of worldwide fame and what became known as Beatlemania!

5. India. For a while, the Beatles were inspired by Indian music and an ancient form of meditation. They traveled to the faraway country of India, where they studied transcendental meditation. During and after this time, they created some of their best music.

ATLANTIC OCEAN
SCOTLAND
NORTHERN IRELAND
REPUBLIC OF IRELAND
George
Paul
John
Ringo
Liverpool
1
MERSEY RIVER
Liverpool
2
Hamburg
ENGLAND
GERMANY
FRANCE
NORTH SEA
WALES
ENGLAND
London
3
N
W
E
S
CELTIC OCEAN
ENGLISH CHANNEL
FRANCE
CANADA
4
USA
New York City
MEXICO
TO THE USA
TO INDIA
CHINA
INDIA
5
INDIAN OCEAN

TIMELINE OF THE BEATLES' LIVES

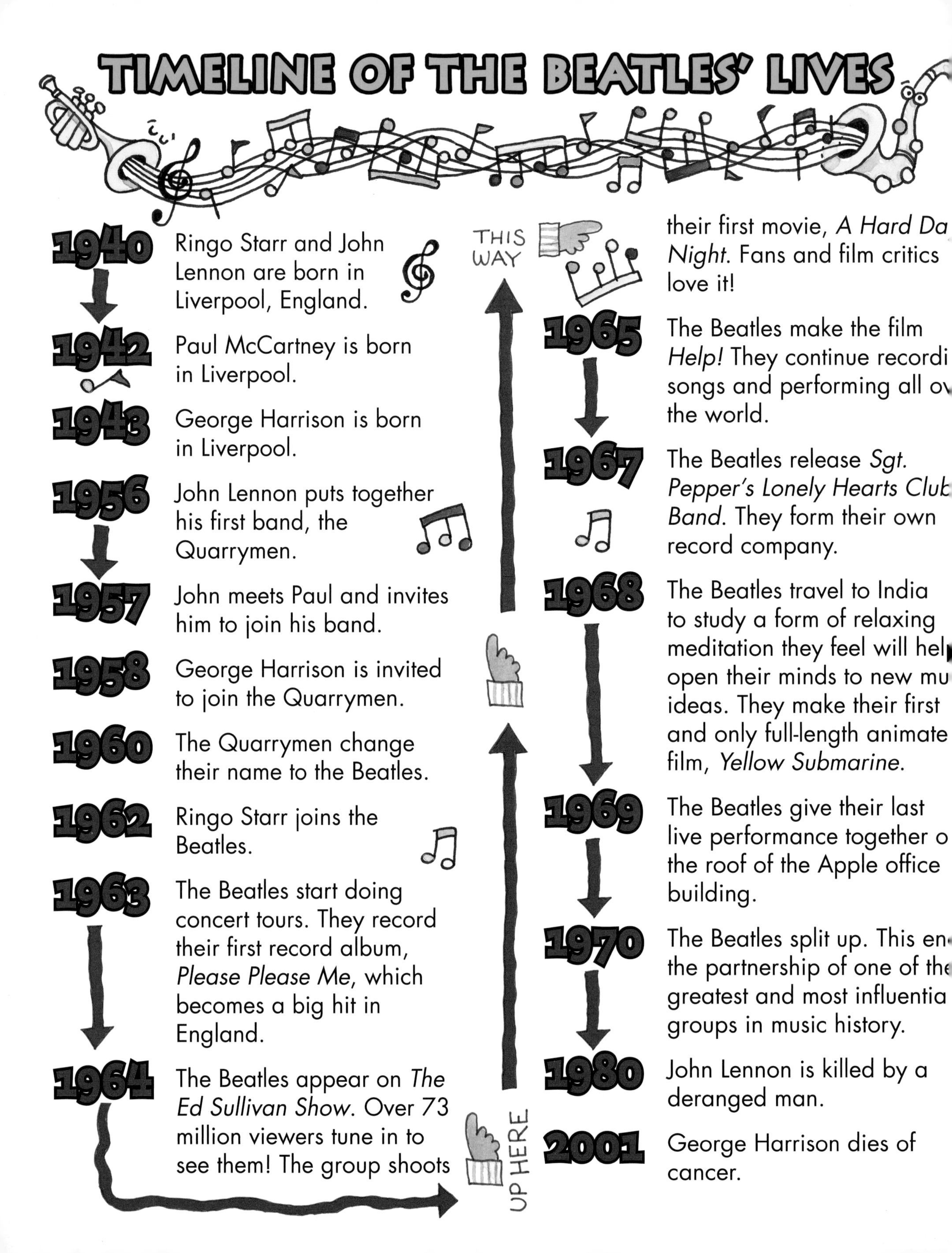

1940 Ringo Starr and John Lennon are born in Liverpool, England.

1942 Paul McCartney is born in Liverpool.

1943 George Harrison is born in Liverpool.

1956 John Lennon puts together his first band, the Quarrymen.

1957 John meets Paul and invites him to join his band.

1958 George Harrison is invited to join the Quarrymen.

1960 The Quarrymen change their name to the Beatles.

1962 Ringo Starr joins the Beatles.

1963 The Beatles start doing concert tours. They record their first record album, *Please Please Me*, which becomes a big hit in England.

1964 The Beatles appear on *The Ed Sullivan Show*. Over 73 million viewers tune in to see them! The group shoots their first movie, *A Hard Da Night*. Fans and film critics love it!

1965 The Beatles make the film *Help!* They continue recordi songs and performing all ov the world.

1967 The Beatles release *Sgt. Pepper's Lonely Hearts Club Band*. They form their own record company.

1968 The Beatles travel to India to study a form of relaxing meditation they feel will hel open their minds to new mu ideas. They make their first and only full-length animate film, *Yellow Submarine*.

1969 The Beatles give their last live performance together o the roof of the Apple office building.

1970 The Beatles split up. This en the partnership of one of the greatest and most influentia groups in music history.

1980 John Lennon is killed by a deranged man.

2001 George Harrison dies of cancer.

GETTING TO KNOW
THE WORLD'S
GREATEST COMPOSERS

THE BEATLES

WRITTEN AND ILLUSTRATED BY MIKE VENEZIA

CONSULTANT
DONALD FREUND, PROFESSOR OF COMPOSITION,
INDIANA UNIVERSITY SCHOOL OF MUSIC

CHILDREN'S PRESS®

An Imprint of Scholastic Inc.

To my sister Debbie. Thanks for reminding me about our 1967 Sgt. Pepper party—"The greatest party of the 20th century."

Picture Acknowledgements
AP/Wide World Photos: 6 bottom right, 6 bottom left, 24, 24 inset; Everett Collection: 3, 8 top right, 8 top left, 11, 14, 17, 19; Globe Photos: 30 (Frank Hermann/Camera Press), 32 (Bruce McBroom), 23 (NBC), 22 (Terence Spencer/Camera Press), 26; Hulton Deutsch Collection Limited: 10, 15, 31; Hulton Getty Picture Collection Limited;21 (Steve Hale Photography), 4 (Bert Hardy); UP/Corbis-Bettmann: 6 top right, 6 top left, 7 bottom, 7 top, 13.

Library of Congress Cataloging-in-Publication Data

Names: Venezia, Mike, author, illustrator.
Title: The Beatles / written and illustrated by Mike Venezia.
Description: Revised edition. | New York, NY : Children's Press, 2017. |
Series: Getting to know the world's greatest composers | Includes index.
Identifiers: LCCN 2016046811 | ISBN 9780531220610 (library binding) | ISBN 9780531222430 (pbk.)
Subjects: LCSH: Beatles--Juvenile literature. | Rock musicians--England--Biography--Juvenile literature.
Classification: LCC ML3930.B39 V46 2017 | DDC 782.42166092/2 [B] --dc23 LC record available at https://lccn.loc.gov/2016046811

Printed in the United States of America 113

1 2 3 4 5 6 7 8 9 10 R 26 25 24 23 22 21 20 19 18 17

The Beatles, shown here on the album cover of *Sgt. Pepper's Lonely Hearts Club Band*, were probably the most celebrated rock group ever.

From about 1964 to 1970, the Beatles were the world's most popular musical group. The Beatles were four musicians from Liverpool, England. They were John Lennon, Paul McCartney, George Harrison, and Ringo Starr. None of them had any real music lessons. They pretty much taught themselves as they went along.

Liverpool in the 1940s

In the 1950s, when John, Paul, George, and Ringo were growing up, Liverpool was a poor, gloomy, seaport city. One good thing going on there was that local sailors returning home from their journeys brought back rock-and-roll records from the United States. People who lived in Liverpool became the first people in England to hear the exciting new music.

Rock and roll grew out of a bunch of different American musical styles, including country western and African American rhythm and blues. Rock and roll had a lot more energy, though, and a wilder sound. The favorite instruments of rock-and-roll groups were guitars, drums, and sometimes pianos and saxophones.

Long before the Beatles met, each of them was inspired by rock-and-roll music. They were crazy about singers like Buddy Holly, Bill Haley and the Comets, Little Richard, the Everly Brothers, Chuck Berry, Jerry Lee Lewis, and especially Elvis Presley.

Jerry Lee Lewis

Chuck Berry

Buddy Holly

Little Richard

Bill Haley and the Comets

It wasn't just the music itself that John, Paul, George, and Ringo loved—the words of rock-and-roll songs made them feel good, too. Teenagers everywhere thought that rock singers understood them and had the same kinds of problems as they did.

Elvis Presley

John Lennon as a young child (right) and with his mother (left)

John Lennon started the Beatles. He was born in 1940 during a World War II bombing raid. John's father left his family when John was only five years old. John's mother, Julia, felt her son would be better off being raised by his aunt and uncle.

John's mother stayed close to him while he was growing up, though. She helped him get his first guitar. Since Julia knew how to play the banjo, she was able to teach John to play his guitar a little.

John Lennon was known as a troublemaker in school. He was always getting into fights and arguments. John was smart, but he never got very good grades.

Later, John went to art college. He was a talented artist, but was really much more interested in playing his guitar and singing. John and his friends would practice their music in empty classrooms during lunchtime and after school. This was the beginning of John Lennon's band, which was briefly called the Black Jacks, then renamed the Quarrymen.

The Quarrymen in 1955

A young Paul McCartney
(at left) with his mother and his brother Mike

Paul McCartney was two years younger than John Lennon. Even though music was always around Paul's home while he was growing up, he wasn't very interested in it until he became a teenager.

Paul's father led a small dance band and played the piano. He also rigged up a set of radio receivers for Paul and his younger brother. Paul heard his first rock-and-roll songs broadcast from far away as he lay in his bed late at night.

When Paul was fourteen, he started picking out his favorite tunes on the piano. He was pretty good at this, and soon was anxious to get a guitar. Once he got his guitar, it seemed like it was all he cared about. Paul practiced in any room he could find—even the bathroom!

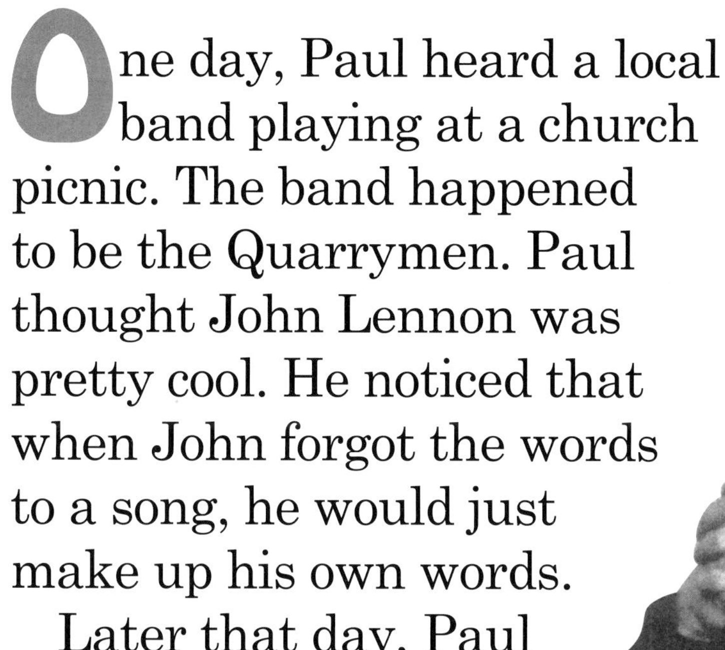

One day, Paul heard a local band playing at a church picnic. The band happened to be the Quarrymen. Paul thought John Lennon was pretty cool. He noticed that when John forgot the words to a song, he would just make up his own words.

Later that day, Paul met John and played guitar for him. Paul imitated some famous rock-and-roll singers perfectly. John thought Paul was pretty cool, too, and asked him to join the Quarrymen.

Paul McCartney

George Harrison was the youngest Beatle. He was born in 1943. Of all the Beatles, George was the one whose parents were the most encouraging when he got his first guitar.

George started out by teaching himself to play. He often became discouraged, and almost gave up. Fortunately, his mother told him he would get it if he kept trying.

Six-year-old George Harrison (at right) with his older brother Pete

George Harrison
at age twelve

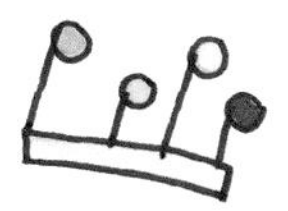

By the time George was fourteen years old, he could play really well.

George happened to go to the same school as Paul McCartney. In fact, George's father drove the bus that took the boys there. George and Paul became good friends. They practiced their guitars at each other's houses. Paul introduced George to John Lennon. At first, John thought George was just a kid, and too young to pay any attention to.

But George had become good enough to get some jobs playing on his own. He kept hanging around the Quarrymen, hoping to become a member. One day, George played a rock-and-roll song that was one of John's favorites. John was so impressed that he said George could finally join the band. Now there were three members of the Quarrymen, who would soon become known as the Beatles.

The last member to join the Beatles was their drummer, Ringo Starr. Ringo's real name was Richard Starkey. He changed his name because he thought it sounded better for someone in show business. Plus, he always wore a lot of rings!

Ringo had a pretty hard time growing up. He was born in 1940, and came from one of the roughest, toughest parts of Liverpool. When Ringo was six years old, he had a serious attack of appendicitis.

Ringo Starr as a child, with his mother

Then Ringo had some other illnesses that kept him in and out of the hospital until he was almost fifteen years old. He fell way behind in school, and had a very hard time catching up. Sometimes Ringo would play in the hospital band, but only when they let him play the drum. As a teenager, he became even more interested in playing the drums, and got a set.

Ringo Starr and George Harrison before Ringo joined the Beatles

Ringo helped start a band that played mostly for the fun of it. Later he joined a band that became very popular in Liverpool. Ringo's new band would usually play in the same places as John Lennon's band, which was now called the Beatles.

The Beatles had a drummer, but John, Paul, and George weren't crazy about him. Sometimes their drummer wouldn't show up, and the Beatles would ask Ringo to sit in with them. John, Paul, and George got along great with Ringo and finally asked him to be their regular drummer.

Now the Beatles had everyone they needed to make a great rock and roll band. John played the rhythm guitar. Paul played bass guitar. George played lead guitar, and Ringo played the drums.

Just before Ringo joined the Beatles, they had been having some luck playing in small clubs in Liverpool and in Hamburg, Germany.

These clubs were dark and dank, and sometimes were filled with creepy customers. The Beatles had to sing for hours at a time, late into the night. To keep themselves from getting worn out, the Beatles ate and drank right on the stage. They often told jokes to each other, and even yelled rude things at their audience! They were having a great time singing songs they had written and goofing around, and their fans loved it.

The Beatles (before Ringo joined them, with Pete Best on drums) on stage in 1961 at the Cavern, a small club in Liverpool

The Beatles, with manager Brian Epstein (top center), after a long evening of performing

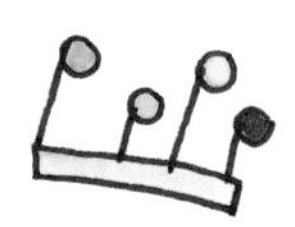

Suddenly, the Beatles were becoming a big hit around Liverpool. Now what they needed was a way to become better known outside of their hometown.

Luckily, a businessman named Brian Epstein came along at this time. Brian ran a record store down the street from where the Beatles were playing in Liverpool. One day, he heard the Beatles, and thought they were great!

Brian met with the Beatles, and convinced them that he could get their songs recorded by a big record company. He also said he would set up concerts, and would try to get the Beatles on radio and TV shows. The only thing Brian asked of the Beatles was to stop goofing around on stage so much, and to dress a little more neatly.

Brian Epstein worked as hard as he could to keep his promise. Before they knew it, the Beatles were playing their music all over England. They even played for the Queen of England! Fans loved the way the Beatles shook their floppy hair around and sang their famous high-pitched "Ooooo." Sometimes it caused some of their fans to faint!

The cheery “yeah, yeah, yeah” you can hear in their song “She Loves You” helped make it the Beatles’ first million-selling record. The Beatles were more popular than ever in England and the rest of Europe. There was one place, though, where the Beatles wanted to become better known.

Opposite page: Wherever they went, the Beatles were mobbed by screaming fans.

The Beatles on *The Ed Sullivan Show* in 1964

John, Paul, George, and Ringo really wanted their music to become popular in the United States—the country where rock and roll began. Brian went to work again. He talked to a famous television-show host in America, and arranged for the Beatles to appear on his show.

On the night the Beatles appeared on *The Ed Sullivan Show*, it seemed like everyone in the United States was tuned in. The Beatles were a huge hit. The only problem was that fans in the audience were screaming so loud with excitement that people could hardly hear the Beatles sing. Now the Beatles were the most popular singing group ever! They began touring all over the world.

Traveling ended up becoming a big problem for the Beatles. Fans kept screaming so much that even the Beatles could hardly hear themselves sing. They always had to rush to and from their hotel rooms so they wouldn't get mobbed. Fans were everywhere! Also, traveling to so many cities all the time started making the Beatles cranky.

Finally, they decided to stop traveling and instead spend more time making records. This is when the Beatles' music started to change in an important way.

In the recording studio, the Beatles discovered and experimented with new sounds that had never been heard before. They used the recording studio kind of like an electronic instrument and created some of the most exciting music ever.

The Beatles tried things like putting echoes on their voices and recording their voices at different speeds. They experimented with the music of India and other cultures. They tried all kinds of different instruments, too. They brought in musicians from important symphony orchestras, and sometimes recorded things backwards. Their music had a huge influence on many rock composers who came after them.

In one of their greatest albums, *Sgt. Pepper's Lonely Hearts Club Band*, you can hear all kinds of wonderful sounds and lyrics the Beatles invented.

The Beatles, with producer George Martin, discuss work during a recording session in 1967. John and Paul composed most of the Beatles' songs, but George and Ringo wrote songs, too.

The Beatles performing the song "Hello Goodbye" in 1967

For the ending of a song called "A Day in the Life," the Beatles made a piano chord last for forty seconds. It sounds spectacular!

By the time the band broke up, in 1970, many people thought the Beatles had done something no other popular band had done. They had made popular rock-and-roll music as important as classical or symphonic music.

By the time the Beatles broke up in 1970, their superb melodies, catchy lyrics, and beautiful harmonies had earned them hundreds of hit songs. Their work had a huge influence on a wide range of rock groups that came after them.

The Beatles split up in 1970 because they each wanted to try doing their own music. They were all very successful. Paul started a new group called Wings. George and Ringo recorded their own music and gave concerts. John wrote music with his wife, Yoko Ono. Sadly, John Lennon was killed by a deranged man in 1980, and George Harrison passed away in 2001, after a long illness.

Today, it's easier than ever to hear the Beatles' music. Their music is on the radio all the time, and you can go online and stream their music for free.

LEARN MORE BY TAKING THE BEATLES QUIZ!

(ANSWERS ON THE NEXT PAGE.)

1. What names did the Beatles use before they called themselves the Beatles?
a. The Quarrymen
b. The Godzillas
c. The Silver Beetles
d. Johnny and the Moondogs

2. TRUE OR FALSE: John Lennon and Paul McCartney wrote music mostly for the Beatles, but every once in a while, they would write hit songs for other groups.

3. As teenagers, all four Beatles loved American rock and roll and skiffle. What is skiffle?
a. A gooey sugarcoated candy made from vegetable by-products.
b. A fun upbeat-sounding music.
c. A popular dance craze where teenagers would group together and dance on giant trampolines.

4. In the Beatles animated film *Yellow Submarine*, who were the bad guys John, Paul, George, and Ringo had to deal with?
a. The Ghoulies
b. Tricloptacons
c. The Blue Meanies

5. What fun nicknames did news reporters and magazine writers give the Beatles?
a. The Shag Heads
b. The Fantastic Four
c. The Mop Tops
d. The Fab Four

6. In 1963, the Beatles recorded *Please Please Me*, their first LP record. What does LP stand for?
a. Long Playing
b. Large Perimeter
c. Loud and Popular

1. a, c, and d

2. TRUE John and Paul wrote a number of songs for other bands, including the Rolling Stones, Peter and Gordon, Gerry and the Pacemakers, Billy J. Kramer, and David Bowie to name a few. John and Paul would sometimes give away their songs to singers who were their friends.

3. b Skiffle was a super-fun style of music that was popular when the Beatles were teenagers. It was a mix of all kinds of music, such as American Blues, country, and folk songs. Skiffle was easy to play and lots of kids started their own skiffle bands, singing together and playing homemade instruments like washtub drums, pots and pans, old guitars, banjos, and almost anything else that made noise!

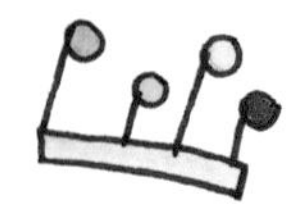

4. c The Blue Meanies not only hated music and color, but anything that was fun! This behavior was something the Beatles were totally against. *Yellow Submarine* featured a lot of the Beatles' best songs, including the title song. Fans could purchase products that went along with the movie too, including Yellow Submarine lunch boxes, puzzles, dolls, stickers, trading cards, posters, and more.

5. c and d

6. a Long before CDs and music streaming, LP records were one of the best ways to listen to your fav music. They were 12 inches in diameter, made of sturdy vinyl, and played about 20 minutes of music on each side. One cool thing that LP records came with were large protective covers that allowed bands to show great art on the front.

HEY, WHAT DOES THAT WORD MEAN?

appendicitis (uh-pen-duh-SYE-tiss) An infection of the appendix, the small tube leading from the large intestine

broadcast (BRAWD-kast) to send out by radio

chord (KORD) A combination of musical notes played at the same time

classical music (KLASS-uh-kuhl MYOO-zik) Music of the European tradition, such as opera, chamber music, and symphony

deranged (di-RAYNJD) Insane or mentally ill

discouraged (diss-KUR-ijd) Having lost enthusiasm or confidence

encouraging (en-KUR-uh-jing) Giving someone confidence by supporting them

lyrics (LIHR-iks) The words of a song

receiver (ri-SEE-vur) A piece of equipment that receives radio signals and turns them into sounds

spectacular (spek-TAK-yuh-lur) Remarkable or dramatic

symphony orchestra (SIM-fuh-nee OR-kuh-struh) A large group of musicians who play together on various instruments, including string, woodwind, brass, and percussion instruments

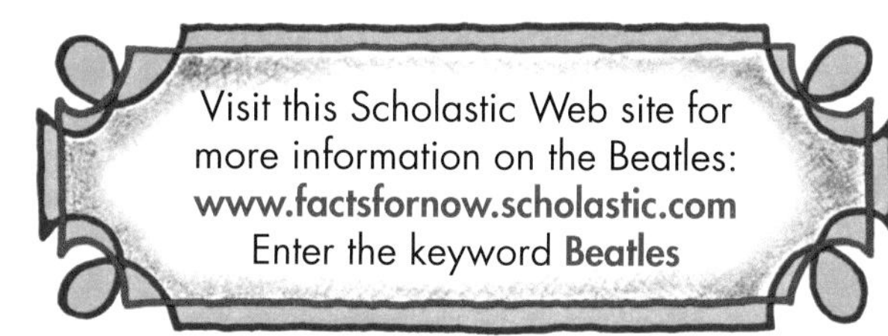

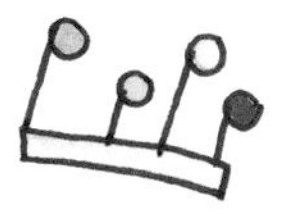

INDEX